Dear Parent:
Your child's love of reading starts here!

Every child learns to read in a different way and at his or her own speed. Some go back and forth between reading levels and read favorite books again and again. Others read through each level in order. You can help your young reader improve and become more confident by encouraging his or her own interests and abilities. From books your child reads with you to the first books he or she reads alone, there are I Can Read Books for every stage of reading:

SHARED READING
Basic language, word repetition, and whimsical illustrations, ideal for sharing with your emergent reader

BEGINNING READING
Short sentences, familiar words, and simple concepts for children eager to read on their own

READING WITH HELP
Engaging stories, longer sentences, and language play for developing readers

READING ALONE
Complex plots, challenging vocabulary, and high-interest topics for the independent reader

ADVANCED READING
Short paragraphs, chapters, and exciting themes for the perfect bridge to chapter books

I Can Read Books have introduced children to the joy of reading since 1957. Featuring award-winning authors and illustrators and a fabulous cast of beloved characters, I Can Read Books set the standard for beginning readers.

A lifetime of discovery begins with the magical words "I Can Read!"

Visit www.icanread.com for information on enriching your child's reading experience.

I Can Read!

BEGINNING 1 READING

Pinkalicious®
and the Sick Day

To all the school nurses
who take care of our children.
Thank you!
—V.K.

The author gratefully acknowledges
the artistic and editorial contributions of
Dynamo and Kamilla Benko.

I Can Read Book® is a trademark of HarperCollins Publishers.

Pinkalicious and the Sick Day
Copyright © 2015 by Victoria Kann

PINKALICIOUS and all related logos and characters are trademarks of Victoria Kann. Used with permission.

Based on the HarperCollins book *Pinkalicious* written by
Victoria Kann and Elizabeth Kann, illustrated by Victoria Kann
All rights reserved. Manufactured in the U. S. A
No part of this book may be used or reproduced in any manner whatsoever without
written permission except in the case of brief quotations embodied in critical articles and reviews.
For information address HarperCollins Children's Books, a division of HarperCollins Publishers,
195 Broadway, New York, NY 10007.
www.icanread.com

Library of Congress Control Number: 2015935855

ISBN 978-0-06-224599-1 (trade bdg.)—ISBN 978-0-06-224600-4 (pbk.)

17 18 19 20   LSCC   10
❖
First Edition

I Can Read!

BEGINNING 1 READING

Pinkalicious®
and the Sick Day

by Victoria Kann

HARPER
An Imprint of HarperCollinsPublishers

When the bell rang

at the end of the day,

Principal Hart handed me a letter.

"Give this to your mom," she said.

Uh-oh. Was I in trouble?

When I got home, I found Mommy.

I waited while she read the letter.

Mommy smiled.

"You have perfect attendance.

Tomorrow you get to be

principal for the day," she said.

"I'm very proud of you!"

"Yippee!" I yelled.

"I'm in charge.

No homework!"

"I don't know about that,"
Mommy said.
"However, you do get to read
the morning announcements
and eat lunch with Principal Hart."

After dinner, I worked on

my announcer's voice.

"Good morning, students," I said.

"Bravo, Pinkalicious," Daddy said.

"You must be very excited.

Your cheeks are all pink!"

12

I nodded.

I was excited,

but I was also very sleepy.

I went to bed early.

When I woke up, my head hurt.

My eyes itched.

My throat felt scratchy.

ACHOO! ACHOO! ACHOO!

Daddy took my temperature.

"You have a fever," he said.

"No school for you today."

He tucked me back into bed.

Then I remembered.

"I HAVE to go to school," I said.

"I'm principal for the day!"

"I'm sorry, Pinkalicious,"

Mommy said.

"I will make you some tea,"
said Mommy.

Daddy tried to cheer me up.

He put my favorite books on my bed.

Then he gave me a big hug,

and I went back to sleep.

I woke up feeling a bit better,

but I still had the sniffles.

I looked in the mirror.

My nose was perfectly pink!

Mommy came in with pink tea.
"My mom used to make this
for me when I was sick," she said.
"It's elderberry tea."
I took a sip. Yum!

I got to stay in my pajamas all day!
Mommy brought me crayons,
and I colored in bed.

I drew a picture
of me riding Goldie to school.

Daddy called from work
to see how I was.
He told me a joke to make me laugh.
"Why did the pink panda
go to the doctor's office?
Because she was pink!"

I giggled, but I was still a little
sad because I wasn't at school.
I would not be able to share
the joke at recess.

In the afternoon, the phone rang.

It was Principal Hart!

"I'm home sick, too," she said.

"When you come back,

you can still

be principal for the day."

I felt a pinka-million times better.

Then Peter came home.

"Guess what I did today?" I said.

"I colored and I read books.
Mommy made me pink tea,
and I didn't even
have to get dressed!"

"I want to be sick, too!" said Peter.

Then he smelled my cold medicine.

"Yuck, forget it!" he said.

I giggled.

The next morning,
my nose was a normal color
and I felt all better.
"Your temperature is normal,"
Mommy said. "You can go to
school today."
"Yay!" I cheered.

When I got to school,

I went straight to the office.

I couldn't wait to tell everyone

the joke about the pink panda!

"Good morning," I said.

"This is Principal Pinkalicious!"